# KINGFISHER
# READERS

level
2

# Where We Live

Brenda Stones

KINGFISHER

First published 2012 by Kingfisher
an imprint of Macmillan Children's Books
a division of Macmillan Publishers Limited
20 New Wharf Road, London N1 9RR
Basingstoke and Oxford
Associated companies throughout the world
www.panmacmillan.com

Series editor: Heather Morris
Literacy consultant: Hilary Horton

ISBN: 978-0-7534-3091-0
Copyright © Macmillan Publishers Ltd 2012

9 8 7 6 5 4 3 2 1

1TR/1011/WKT/UNTD/105MA

A CIP catalogue record for this book is available from the British Library.

Printed in China

## Picture credits

The Publisher would like to thank the following for permission to reproduce their material. Every care has
been taken to trace copyright holders. However, if there have been unintentional omissions or failure to trace
copyright holders, we apologize and will, if informed, endeavour to make corrections in any future edition.
Top = t; Bottom = b; Centre = c; Left = l; Right = r.
Cover Shutterstock/June Marie Sobrito; Pages 4 Photolibrary/Uppercut Images; 5t Photolibrary/Asia
Image Group; 5b Photolibrary/GoGo; 6 Shutterstock/Elena Elisseeva; 7t Shutterstock/Felix Mizionikov;
7b Shutterstock/LianeM; 8 Shutterstock/SF photo; 9t Shutterstock/Darko Zeljkovic; 9b Photolibrary/Flirt
Collection; 10–11 Getty/Panoramic Images; 11t Corbis/Adam Woolfitt; 11b Photolibrary/Lineair; 12 Getty/
Image Bank; 13 Corbis/Danny Lehman; 14 Shutterstock; 15t Photolibrary/Age Fotostock; 15b Alamy/
Thomas Cockrem; 16 Shutterstock/prism88; 17t & 17b Nutshell Media /Sue Cunningham; 18t Shutterstock/
Kruchankova Maya; 18b Shutterstock/John Leung; 19 Shutterstock/Vladimir Melnik; 20 Corbis/John Miller/
Robert Harding World Imagery; 21 Shutterstock/Sergii Korshun; 22–23 Shutterstock/kirych; 23t Photolibrary/
Ingram Publishing; 23b Corbis/Lindsay Hebberd; 24–25 Corbis/VStock LLC/Tetra Images; 24t Shutterstock/
Dmitrijs Bindemanis; 26–27 Photolibrary/Bios; 27 Shutterstock/Robert Hackett; 28–29 Photolibrary/Jon
Arnold Travel; 29t Corbis/Pascal Deloche/Godong; 30t Shutterstock/Jose Wilson Araujo; 30b Corbis/Michael
S. Yamashita; 31t Corbis/Gavin Heller; 31c Photolibrary/Photononstop; 31b Shutterstock/Lance Bellers.

# Contents

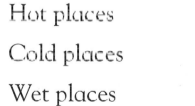

# Where do we live?

We live in homes. Our home gives us **shelter** from the rain and sun. Our home is where we keep our things.

Our home is where we eat and sleep. Our home is where we are safe.

# Houses and flats

There are lots of different kinds of homes. Many people live in houses.

Some houses are joined together in a row.

Others stand on their own.

Some buildings contain lots of homes. These are called **flats**. People have to walk up stairs or go in a lift to get to their flat.

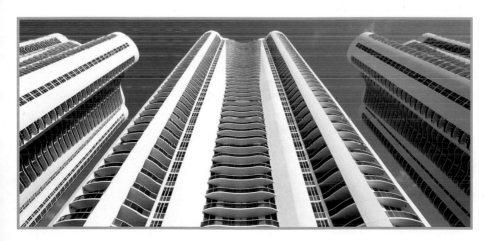

# In a town

When lots of homes are built near each other, the place grows into a town or city. People live close to their work, schools and shops.

The good thing about a town is that your friends are nearby and there are lots of things to do.

# In the countryside

Some people live in the countryside. They may live in homes far from each other. This farmhouse is far from other homes.

Other people live in villages. These are small groups of homes and other buildings.

# Beside rivers

Many towns and cities are built next to rivers. In the past, people used the rivers for cooking, washing and to get around.

Some people still use rivers for washing clothes.

Venice is a town built on **canals**, so people have to travel by boat.

# Beside the sea

Many people live by the sea. They may catch and sell fish, or they may help **tourists** on holiday.

Some people live in houses on **stilts**.
Others live on **houseboats**.

# Made of wood

Houses are made of different materials. Some houses are made of wood because there are lots of trees growing nearby.

This wooden house has a roof of **thatch**. The thatch is made of palm leaves from the forest around the house.

There is no glass in the windows because it never gets cold.

# Made of brick

Bricks are made by baking clay.
Bricks are stuck together with
**mortar** to make walls.

Where it's hot, bricks are made by baking mud in the sun. This amazing **palace** in Yemen was built out of mud bricks.

# Hot places

In places where it is very hot, our homes help keep us cool.

People put **shutters** on the windows to keep out the sun.

They have pools of water and fountains to make the air cool.

In Greece, people paint their houses white to help keep them cool.

# Cold places

In places where it snows a lot, people build their houses with thick walls and roofs to keep out the cold.

They make fires with wood or gas to keep the house warm.

# Wet places

In places where it rains a lot, houses need sloping roofs so the rain runs off quickly.

If it rains too much, the rivers get full of water and there may be floods.

# Dry places

In places where it's very dry, people get water from a well in the ground.

Some people save
rainwater in a
tank when it rains.

# On the move

Some people live in tents like this.
When they move, they carry their
home with them.

Some people live in caravans like this. When they move, they drive their home with them.

# Which home?

Which home did you like best in this book? Was it in a town or in the countryside?

Was it a flat or a palace, a boat or a tent? You choose!

# Glossary

**canal**  a waterway made by digging

**flat**  a small home that is part of a bigger building

**houseboat**  a boat that people live on as their home

**mortar**  a mix of sand and cement

**palace**  a splendid building where kings, queens or other rulers live

**shelter**  a building that protects us from the weather

**shutters**  covers for windows to keep out the sun

**stilts**  legs that hold a house up above the water

**thatch**  a roof made of leaves or straw

**tourists**  people who are on holiday in a place